My name is

....

My body

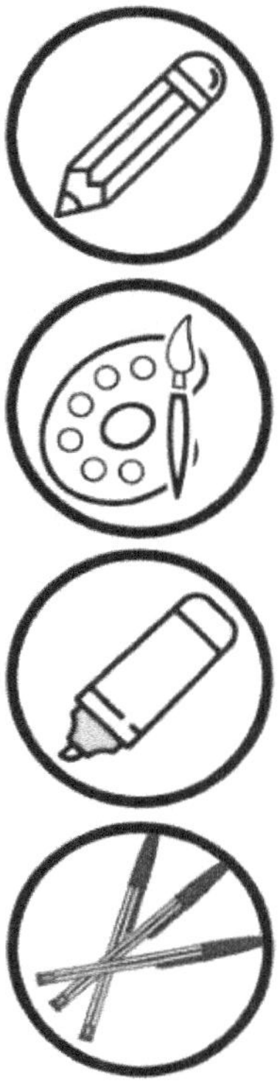

My body
Aula
Creativa

My name is

....

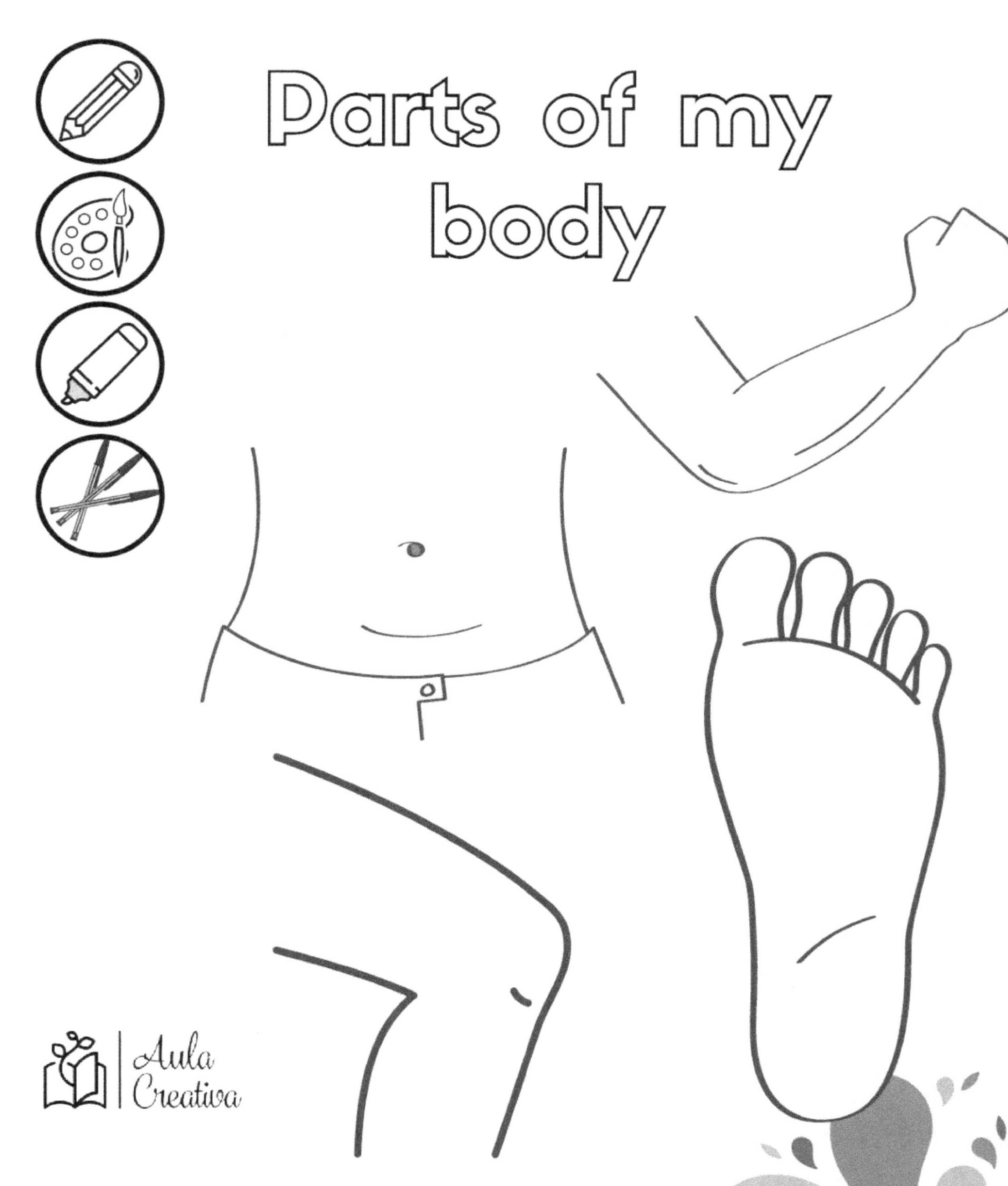

My name is

....

My city

My name is

....

My city

My name is

....

My city

Aula Creativa

My name is

My city

My name is

....

My city

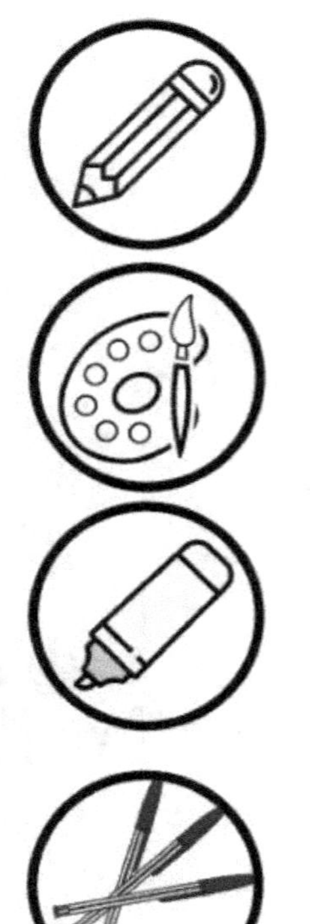

My name is

....

My city

....

My city

My name is

....

My city

My name is

....

My city

My name is

....

My city

My name is

....

My city

My name is

....

My city

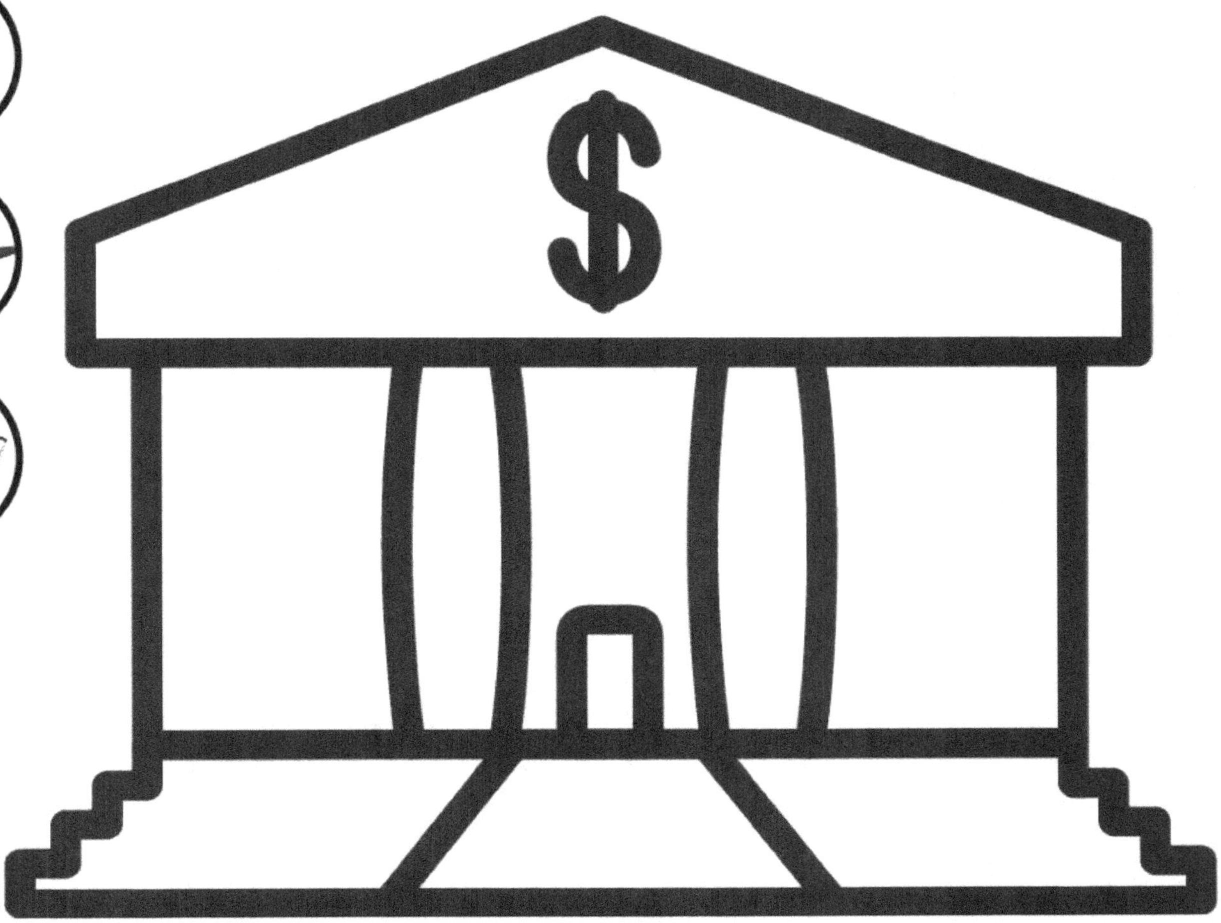

Aula
Creativa

....

My city

My city

My name is

....

My city

My name is

....

My name is

....

My city

My name is

....

My city

My name is

....

My city

....

My city

My name is

....

My city

My name is

....

My city

My city

My name is

. . . .

My name is

Beach

Aula
Creativa

My name is

Countryside

Aula Creativa

My name is

Countryside
Aula Creativa

My name is

Countryside

Aula
Creativa

My name is

....

Countryside

Countryside

My name is

Countryside
Aula Creativa

My name is

....

My name is

....

Countryside

My name is

Countryside
Aula
Creativa

....

Countryside

My name is

The School

The School

My name is

....

The School

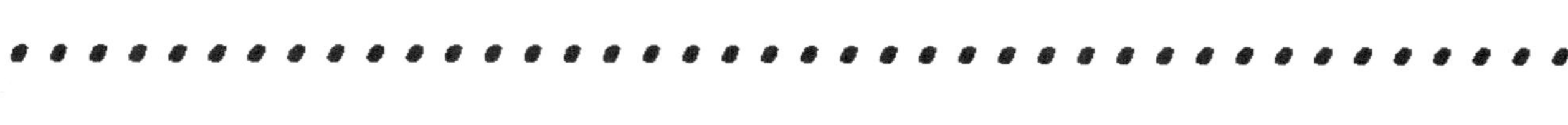

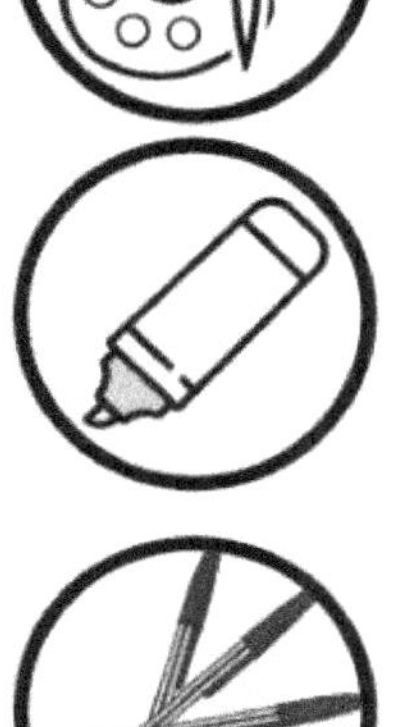

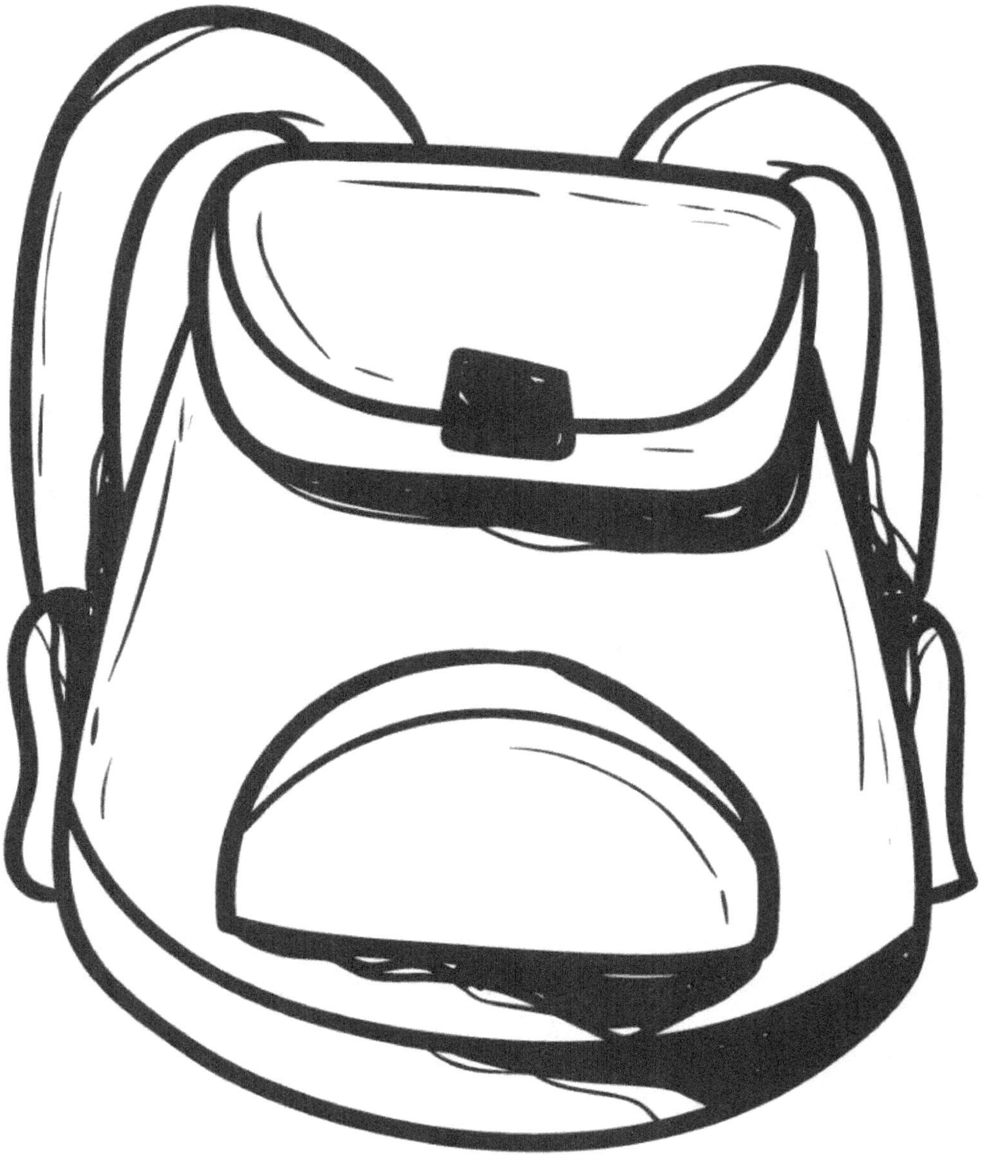

Aula Creativa

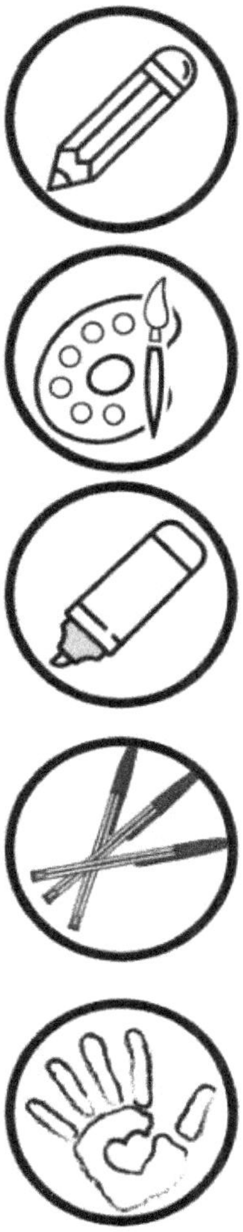

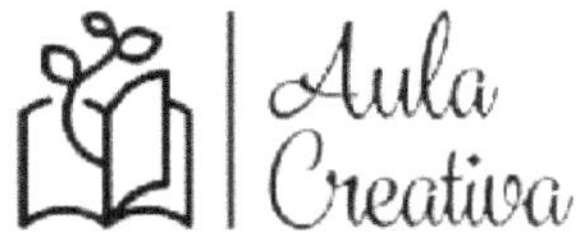

My name is

....

The School

....

The School

My name is

The School

My name is

....

The School

My name is

....

My name is

....

My name is

....

My name is

....

My name is

....

My name is

....

My name is

....

My name is

My name is

Aula
Creativa

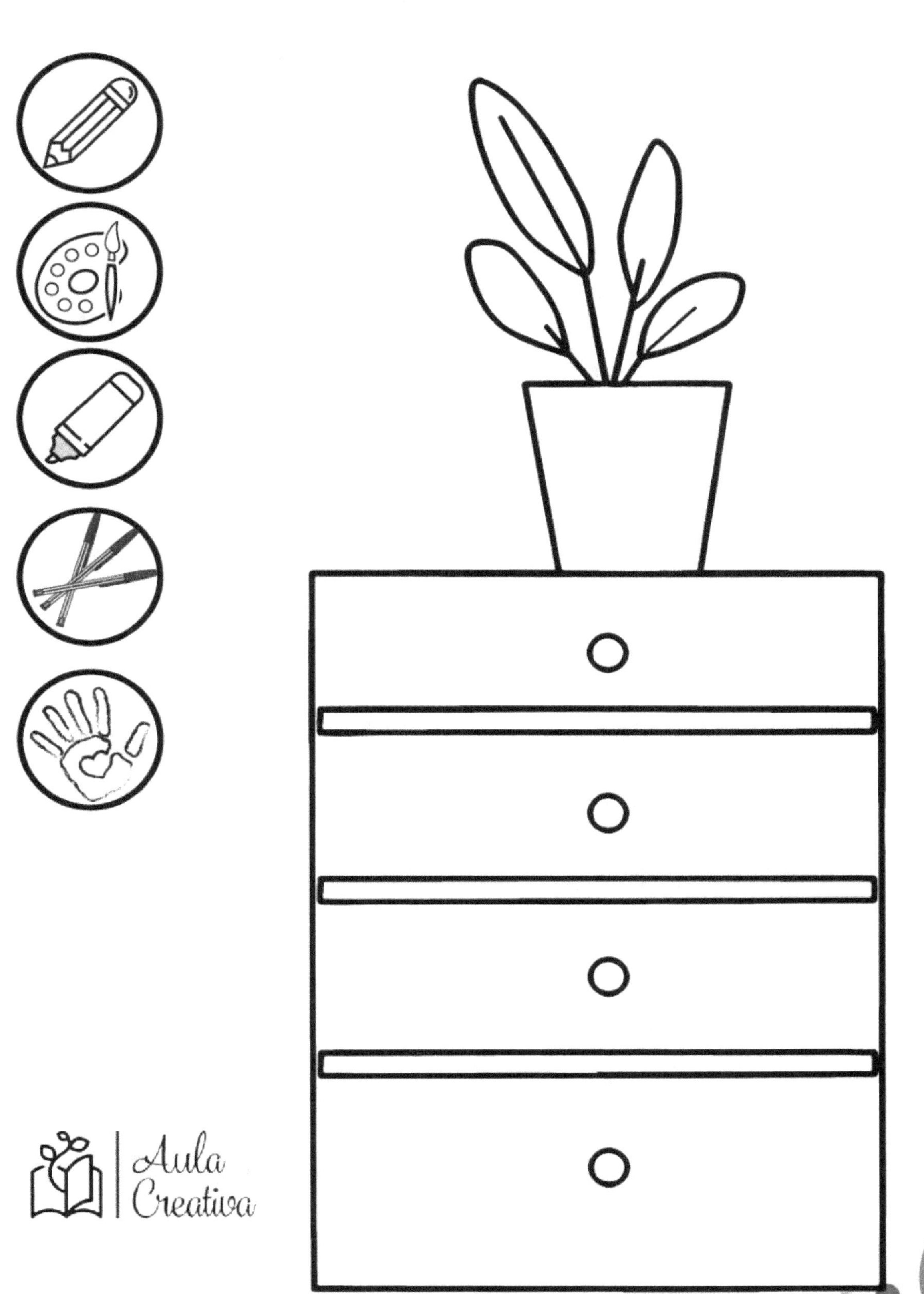

Aula
Creativa

My name is

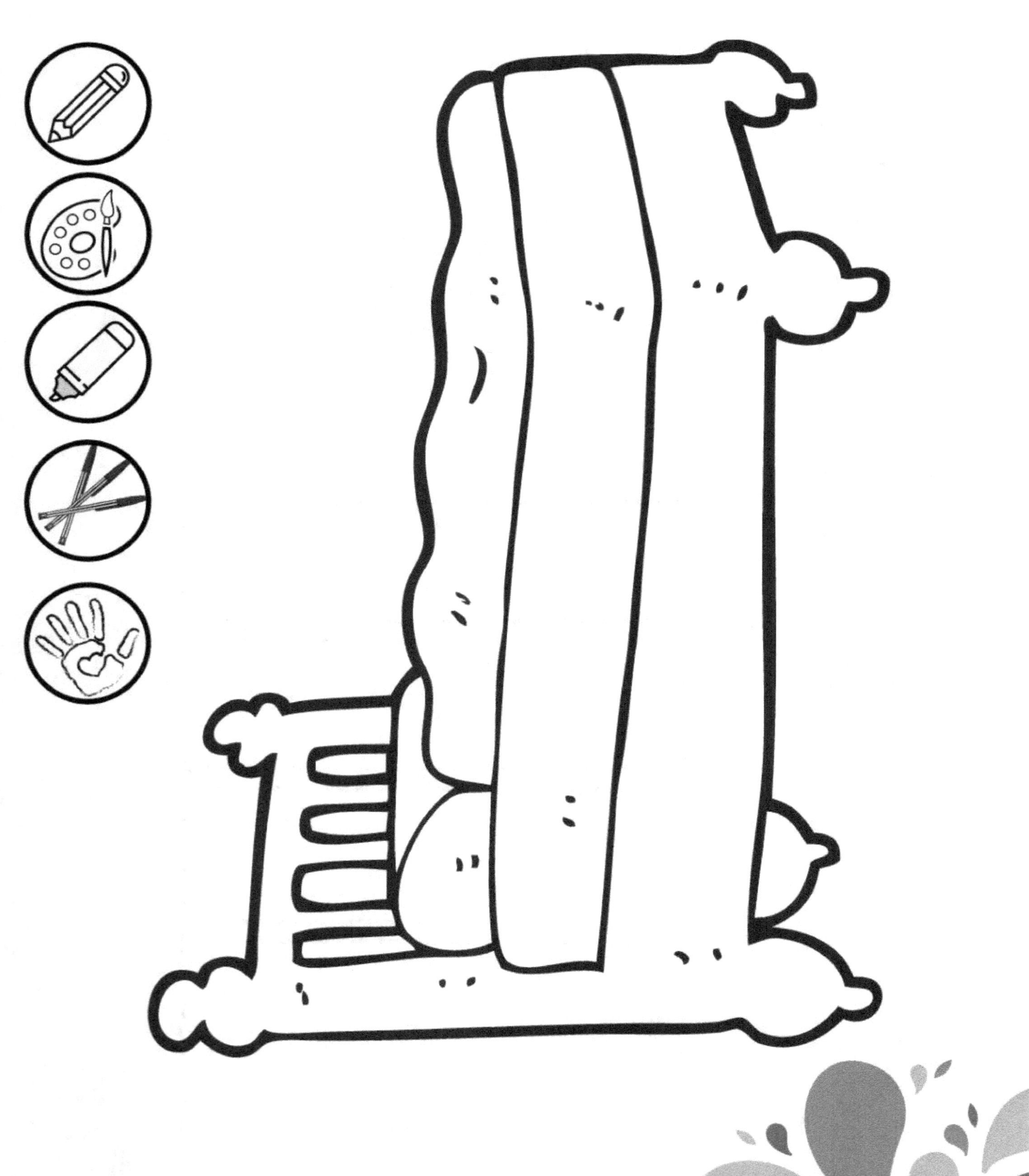

My name is

....

My name is

....

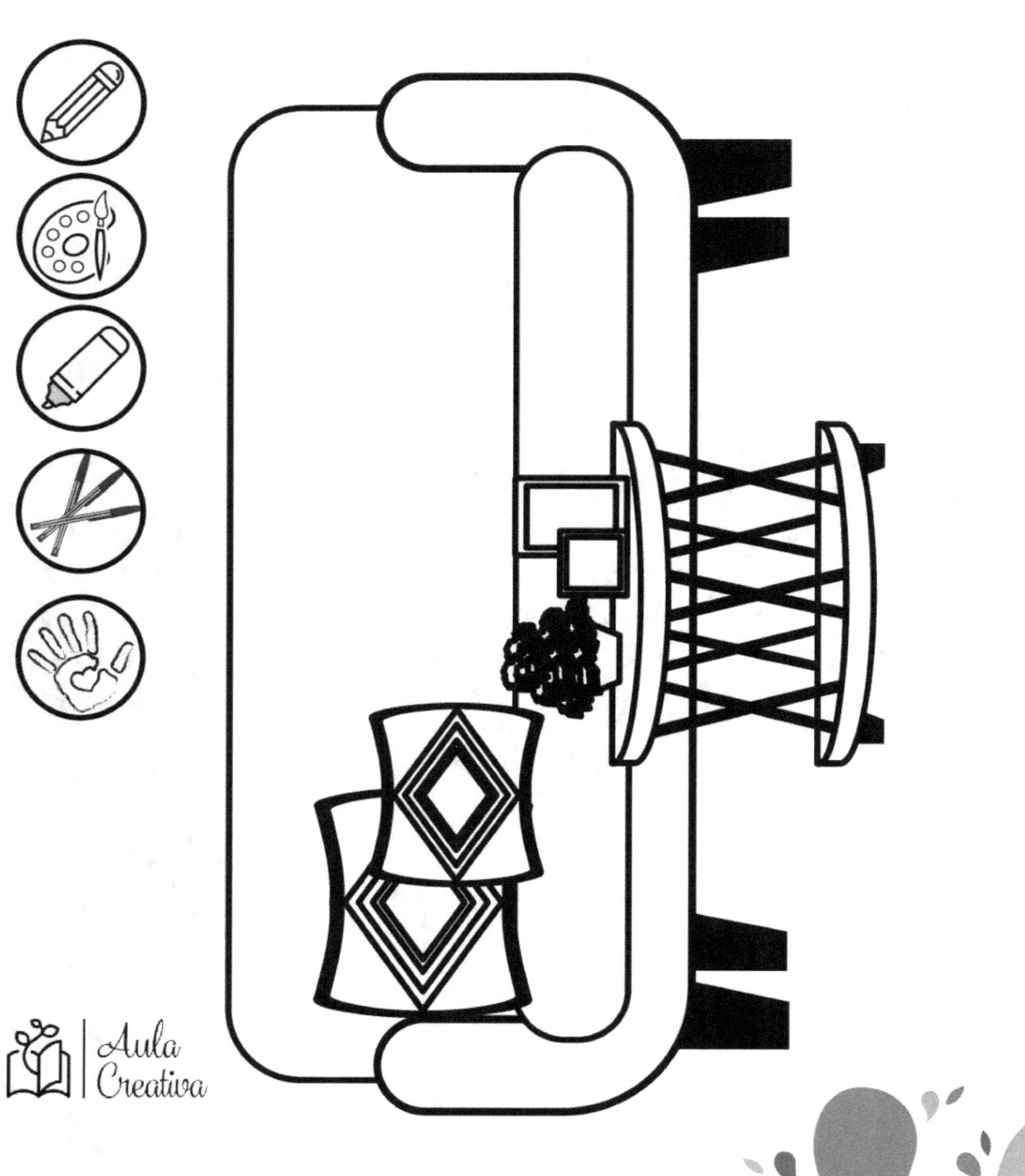

My name is

My name is

....

My name is

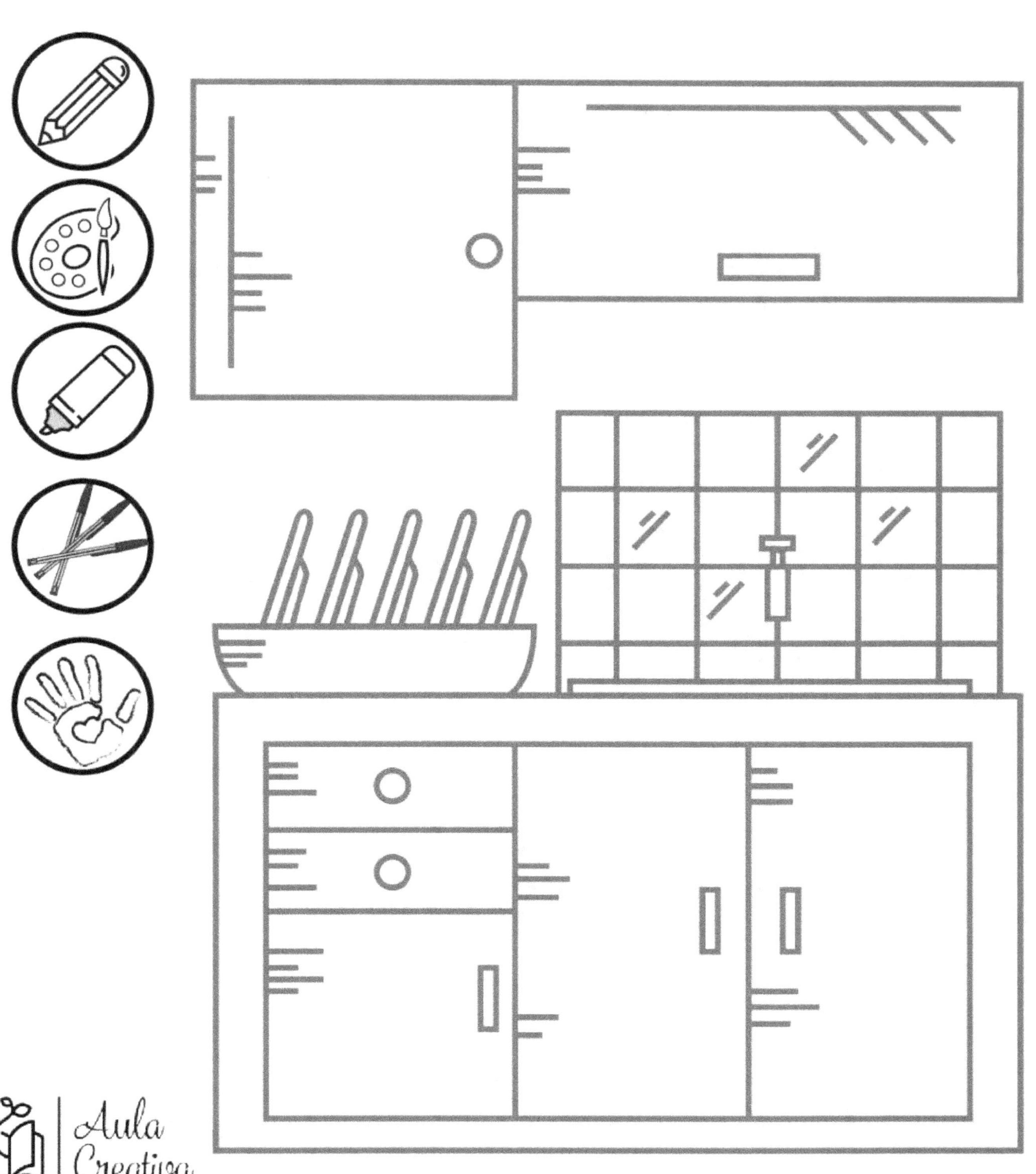

My name is

....

My name is

....

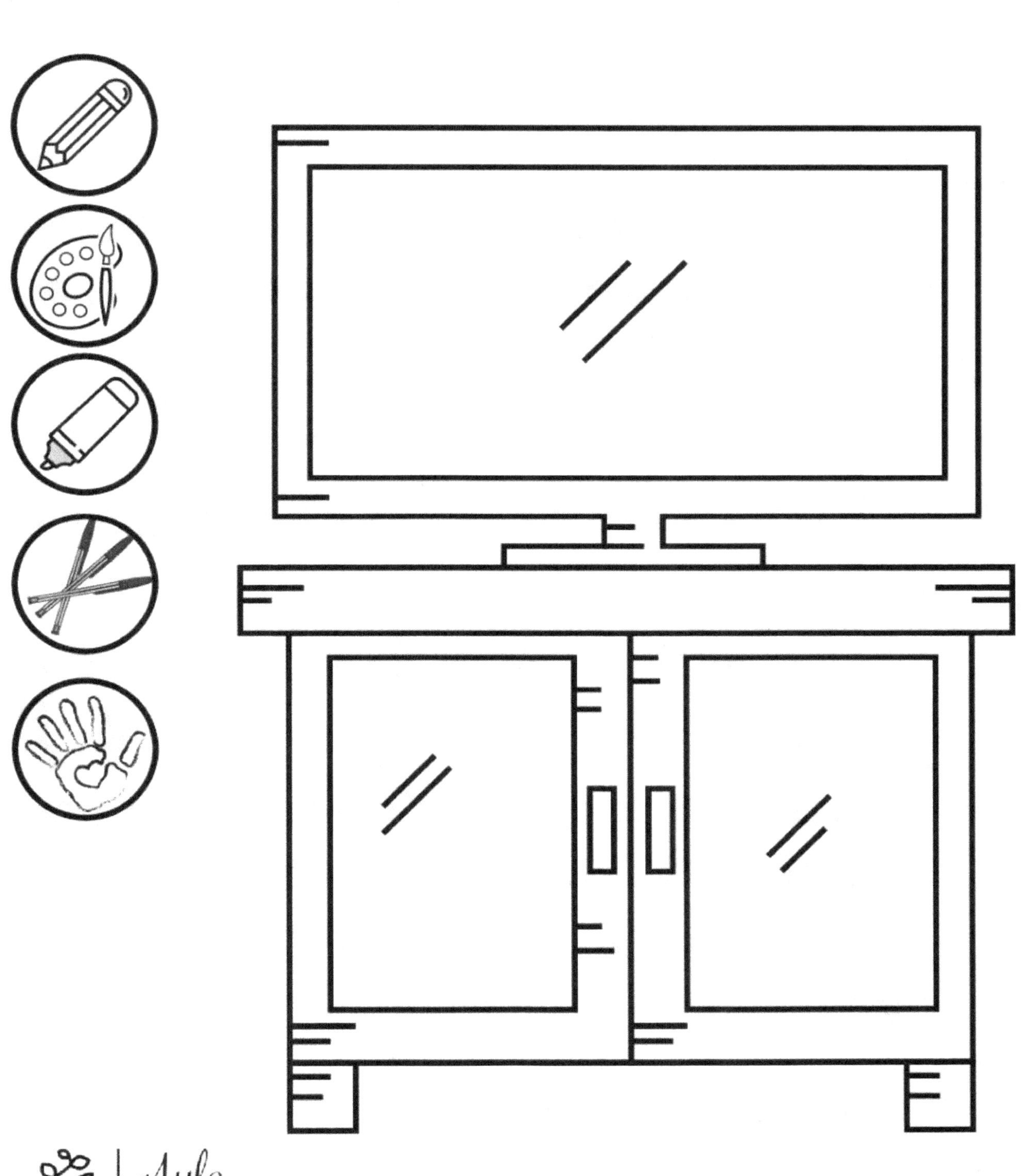

My name is

....

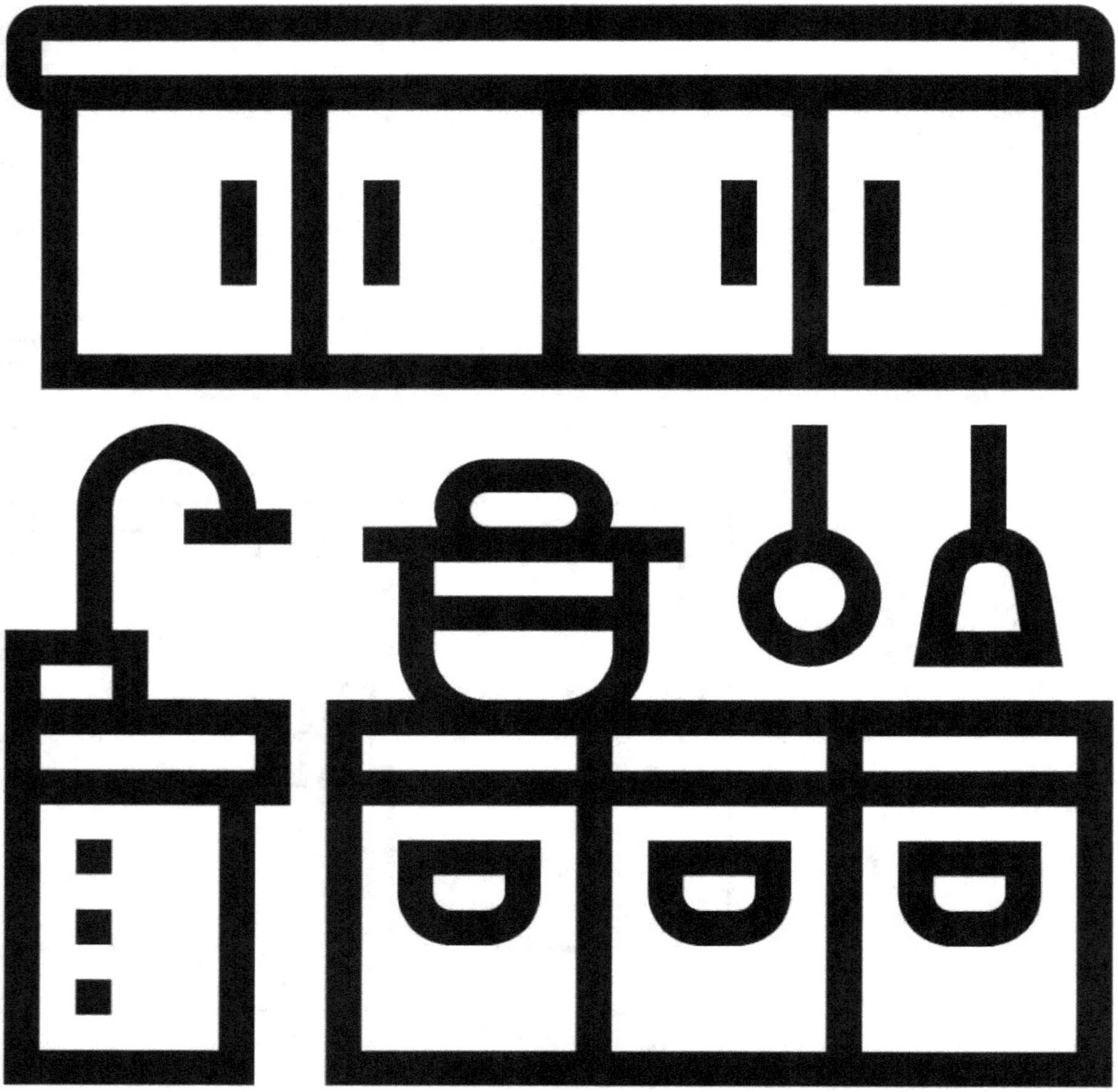

My name is

....

My name is

....

My name is

....

My name is

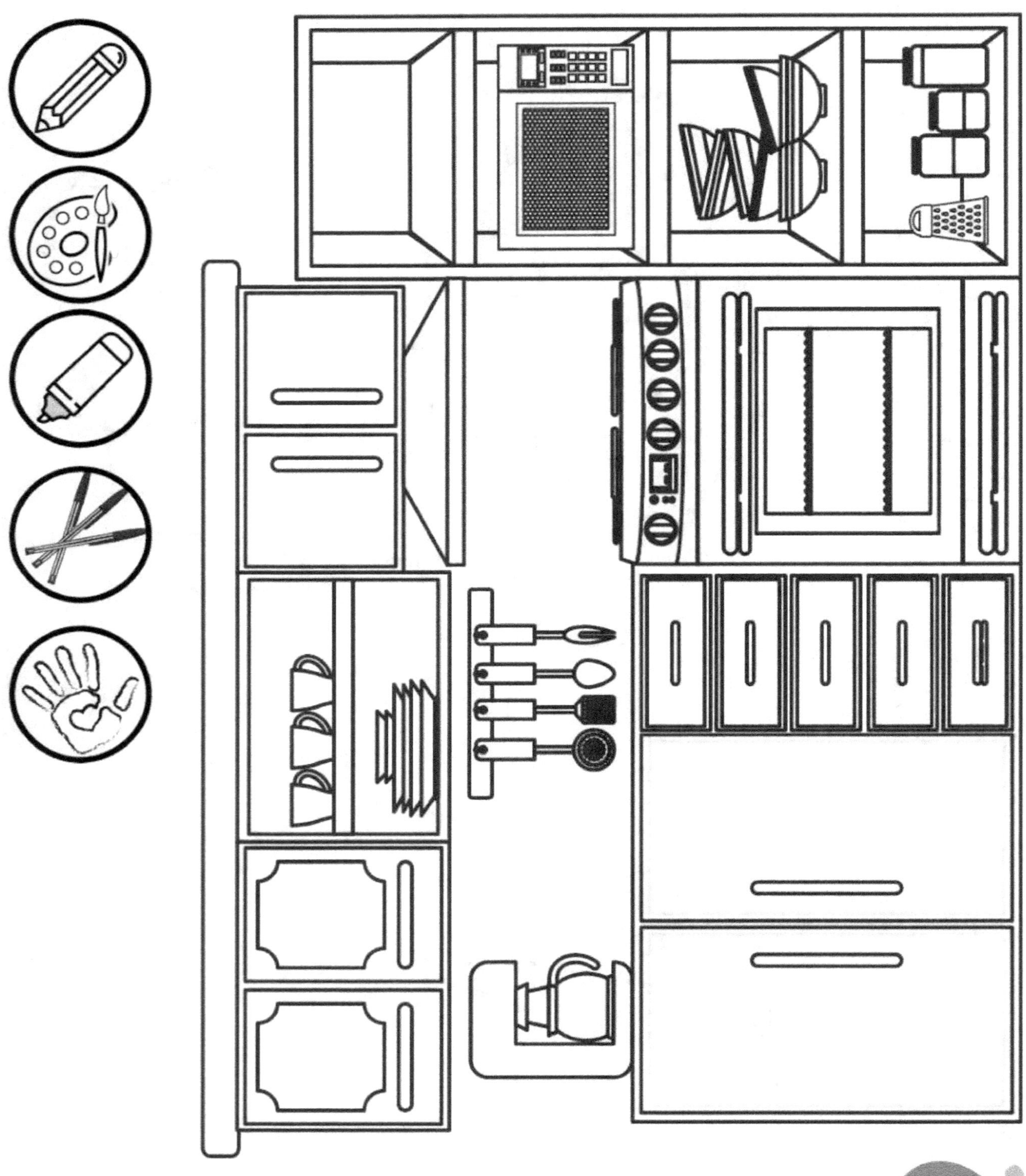

My name is

....

My name is

My name is

....

My name is

....

My name is

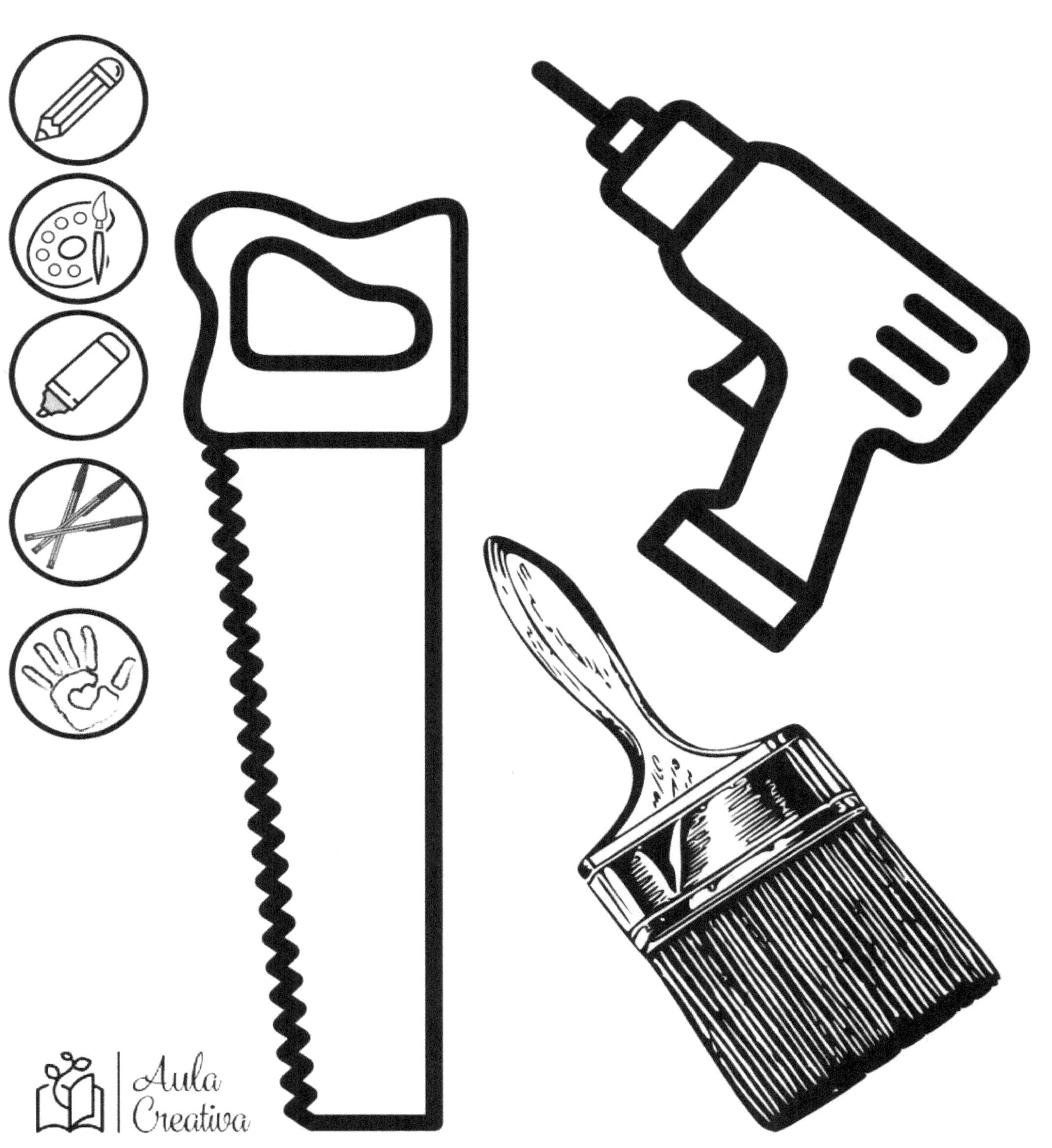

....

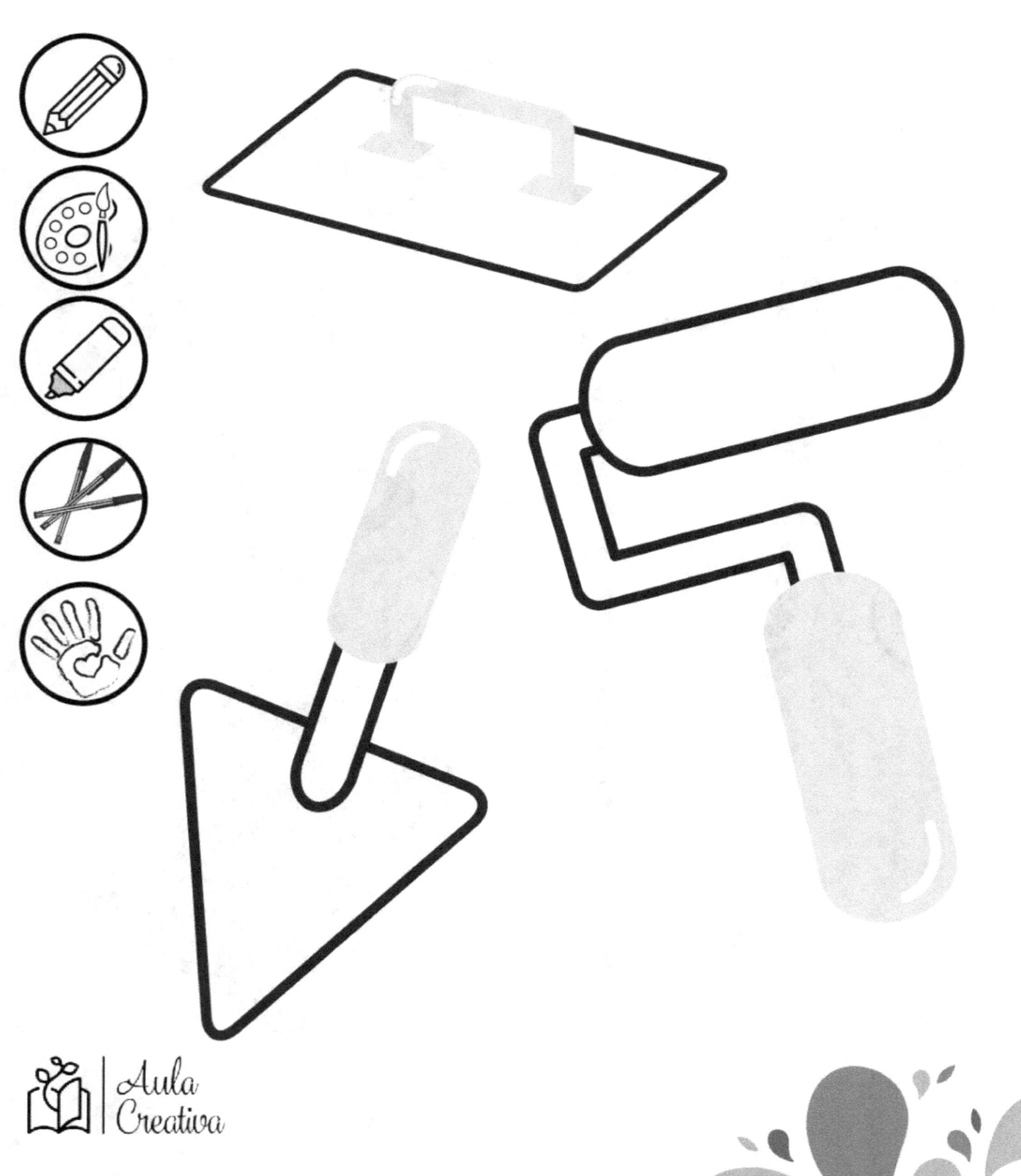

My name is

....

My name is

....

My name is

My name is

....

My name is

....

My name is

....

My name is

....

My name is

....

My name is

My name is

....

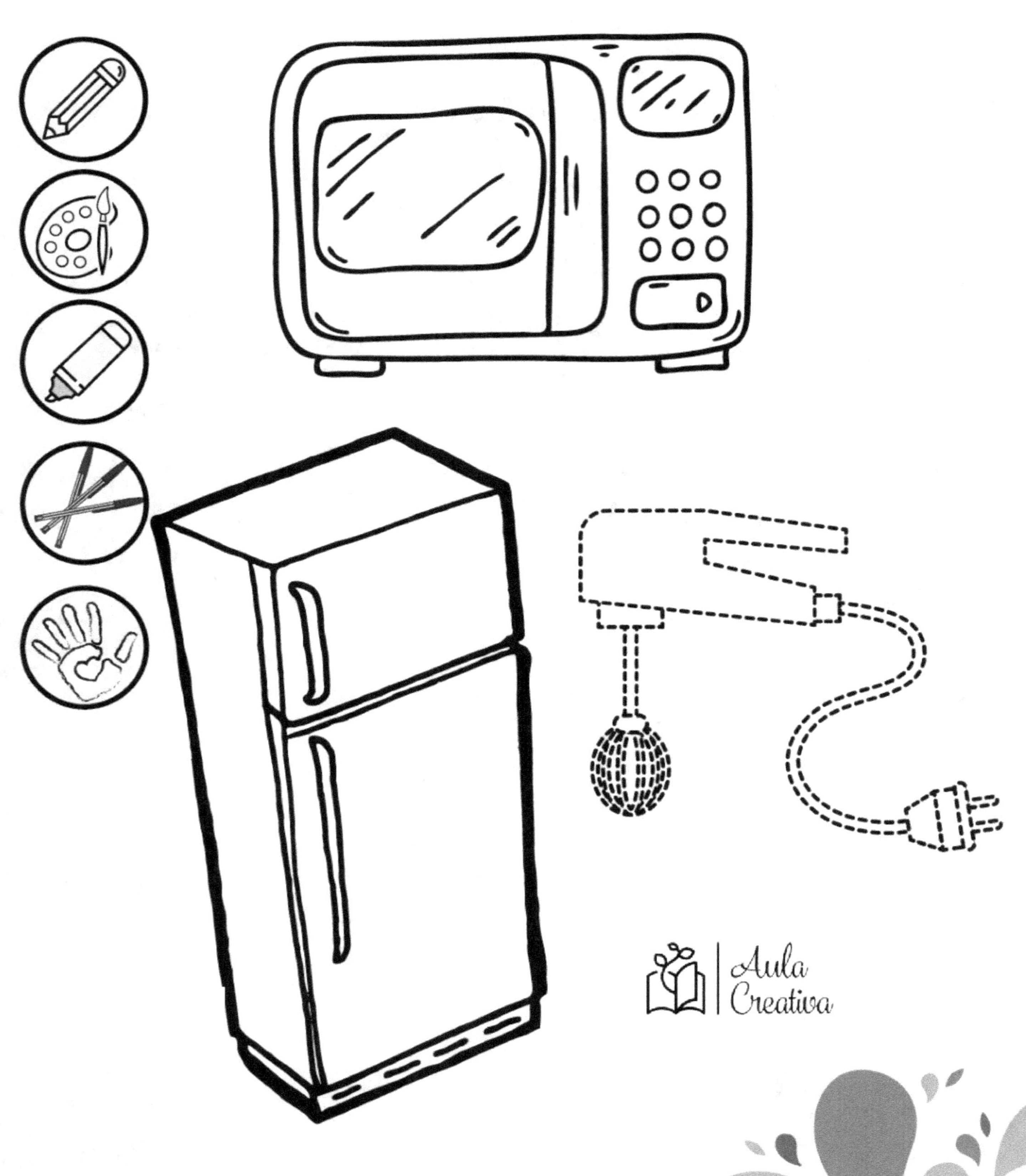

My name is

....

My name is

....

My name is

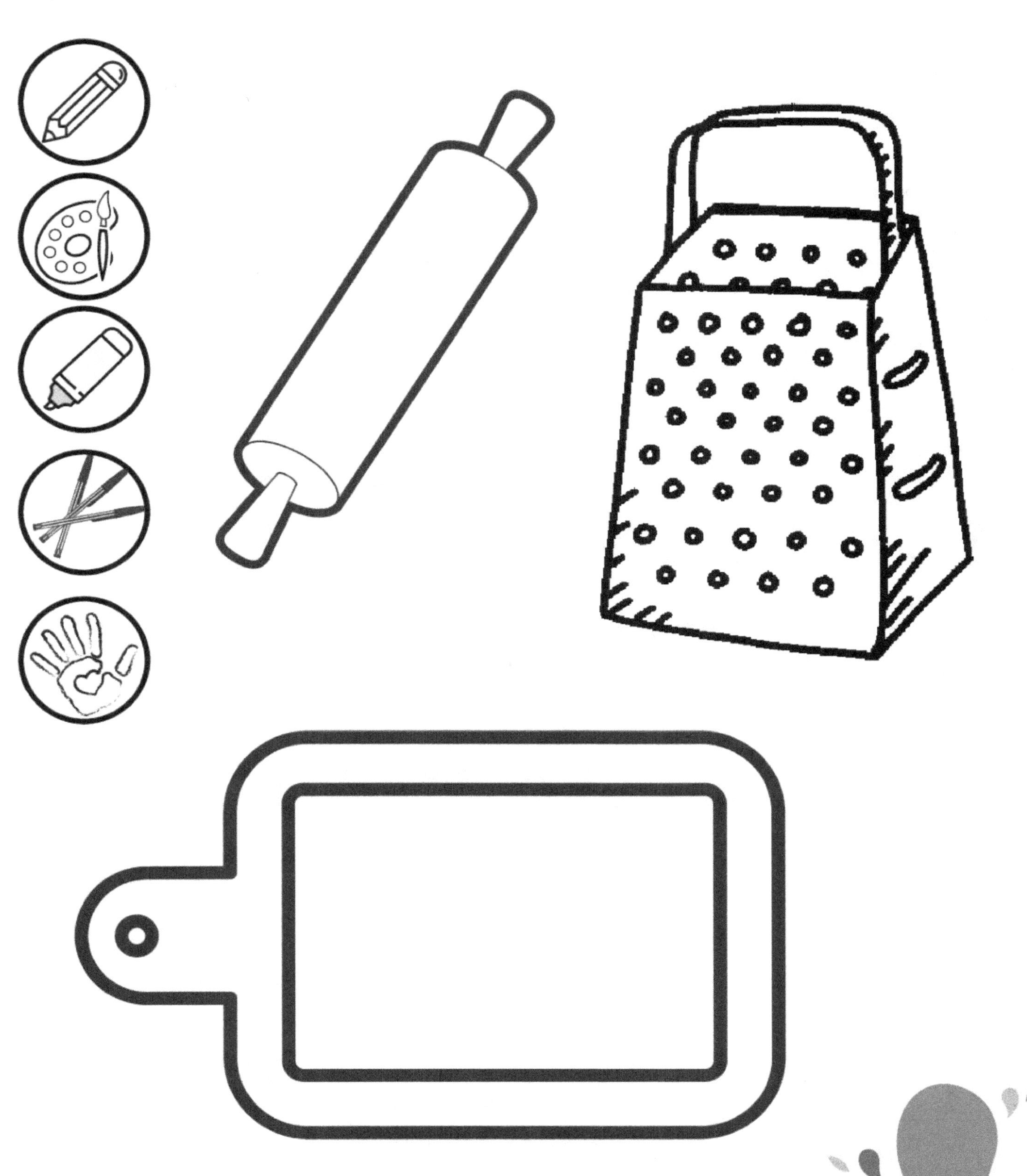

My name is

....

My name is

....

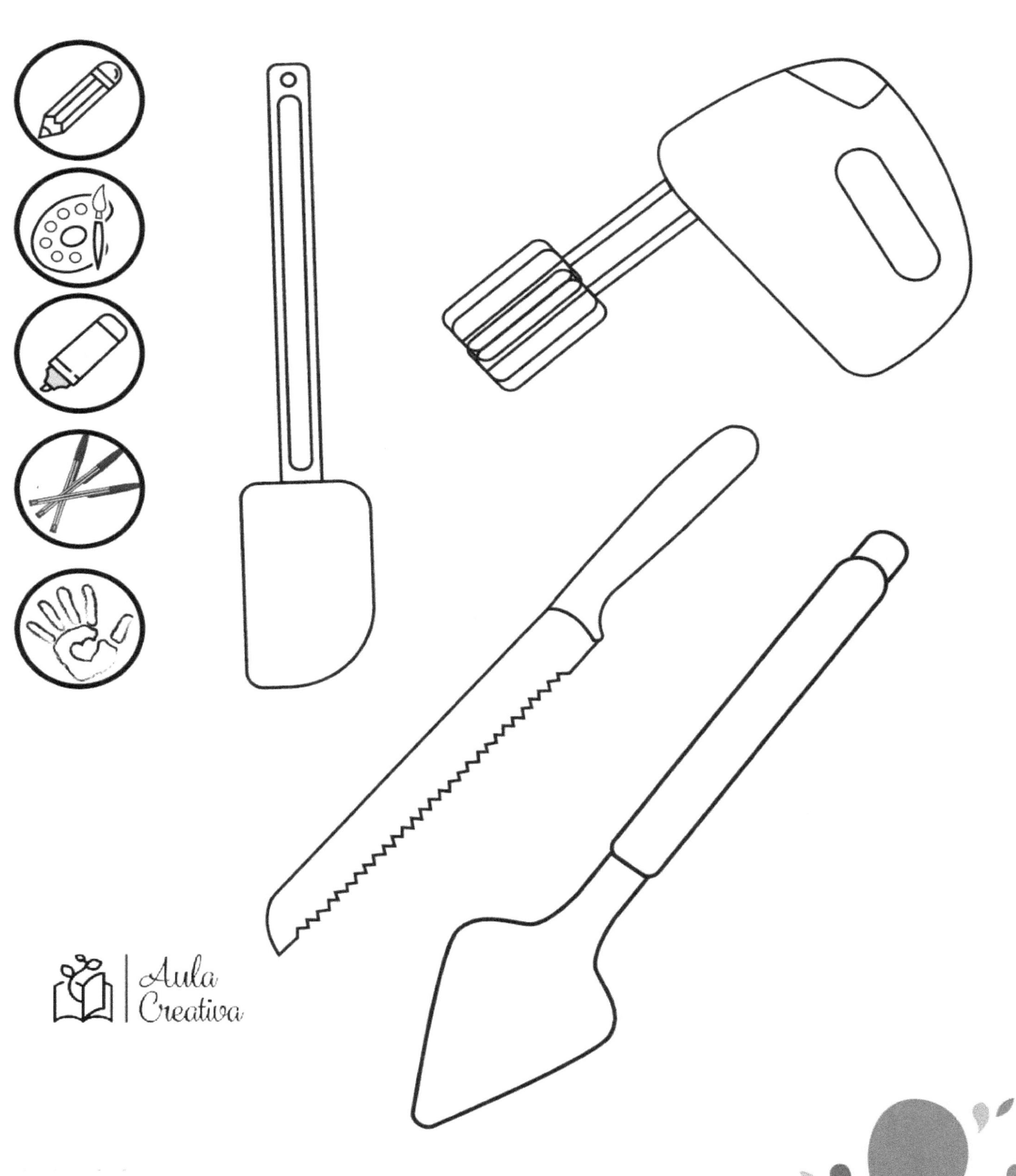

My name is

My name is

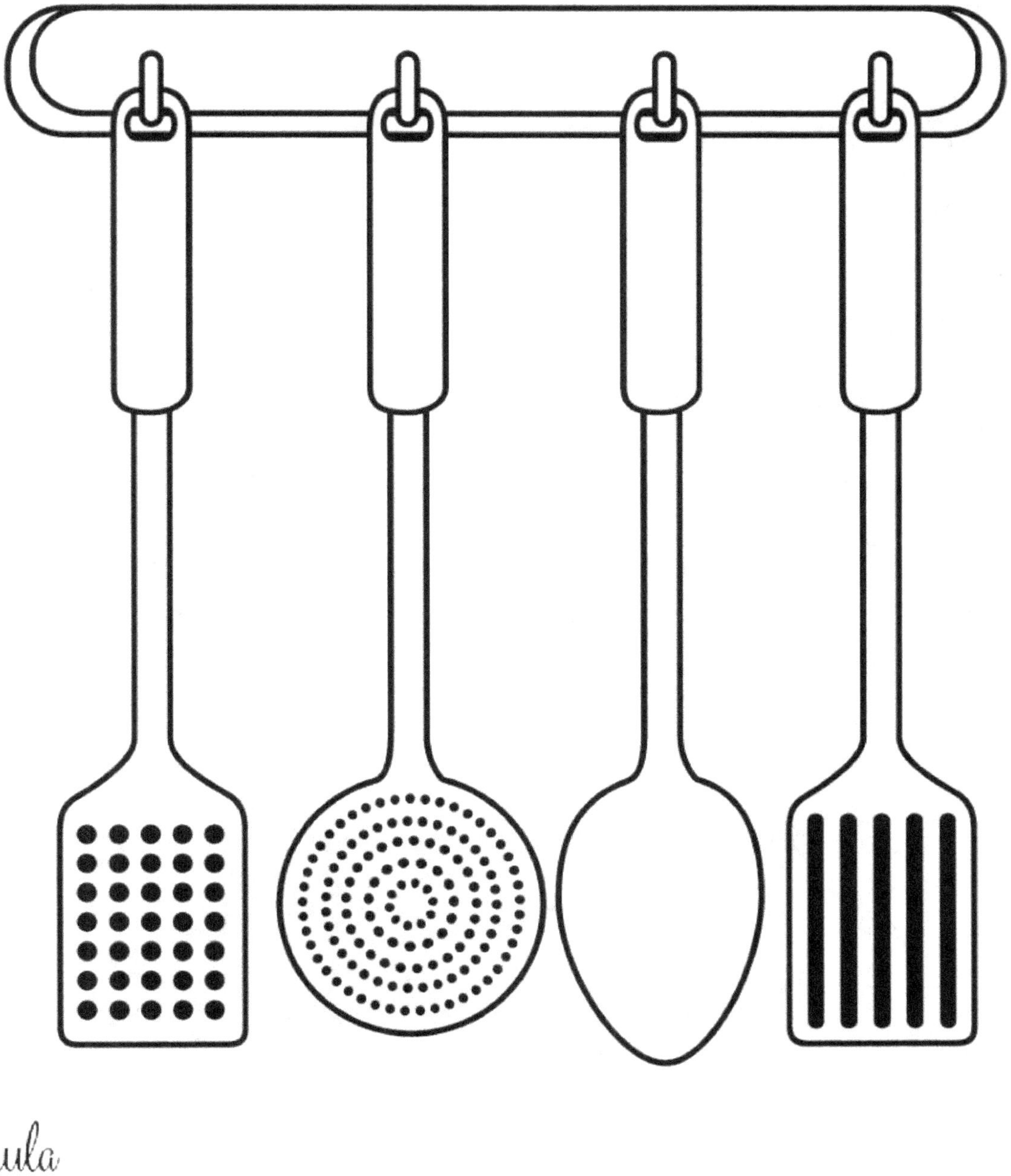

....

My name is

....

My name is

....

Aula Creativa

My name is

....

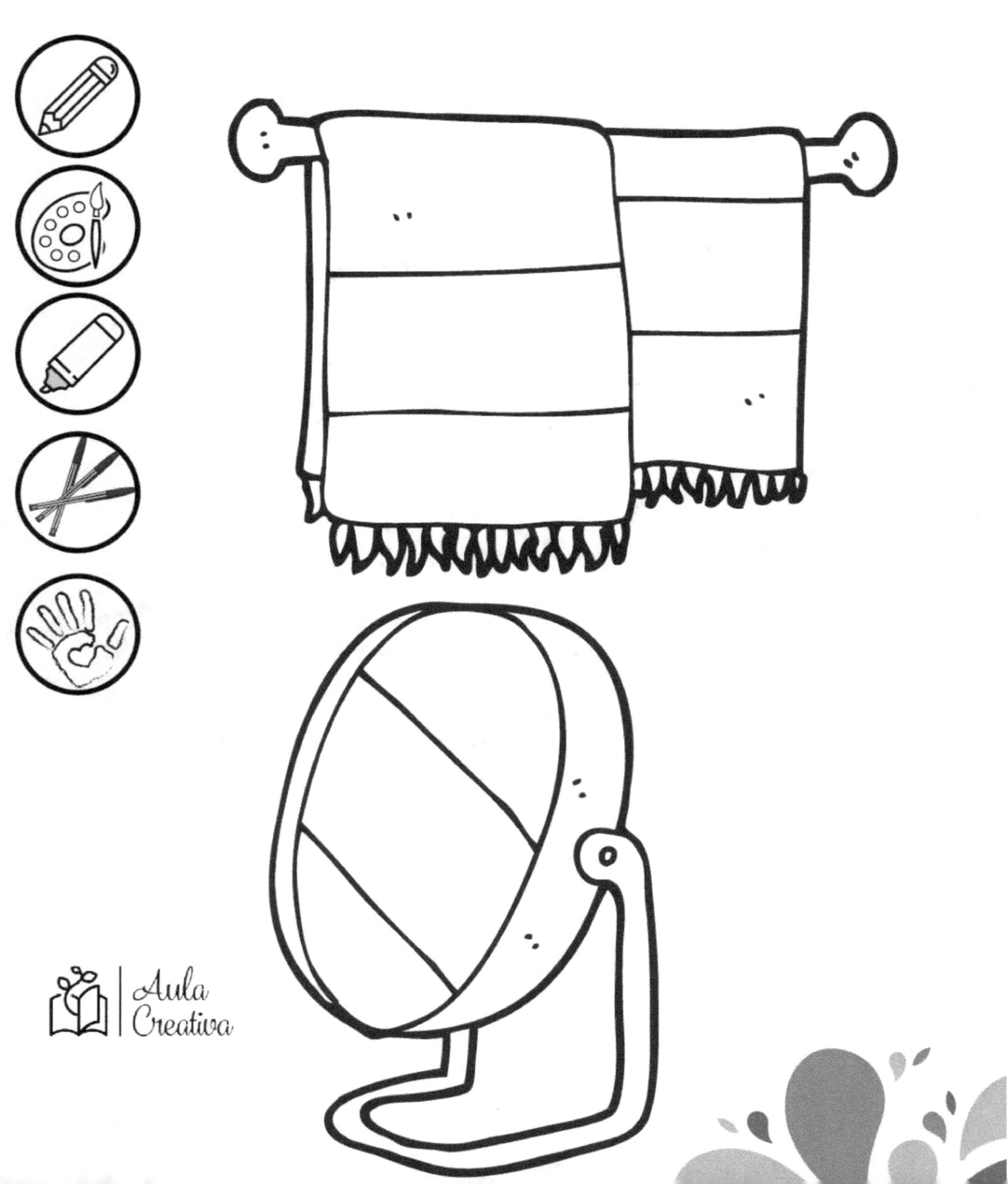

My name is

....

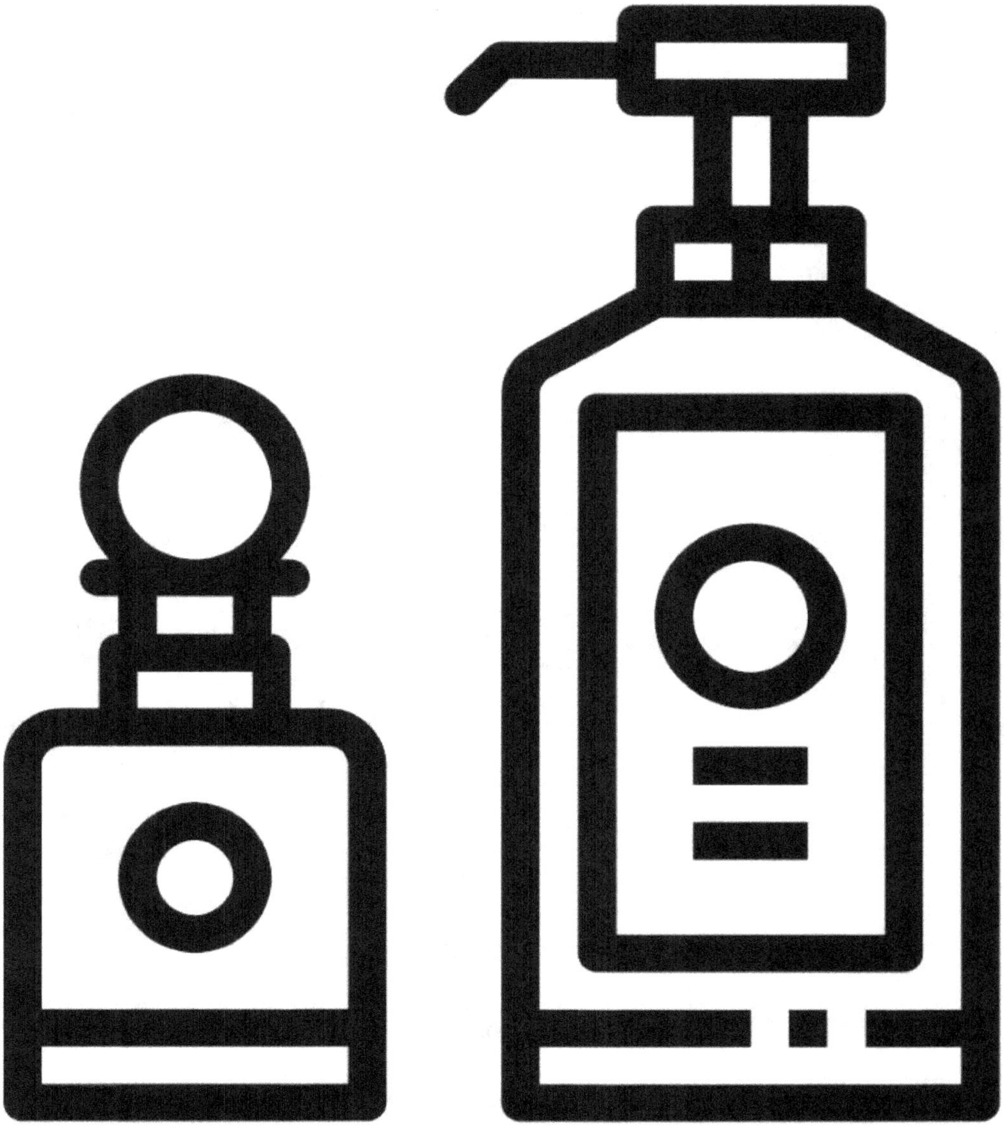

My name is

....

My name is

....

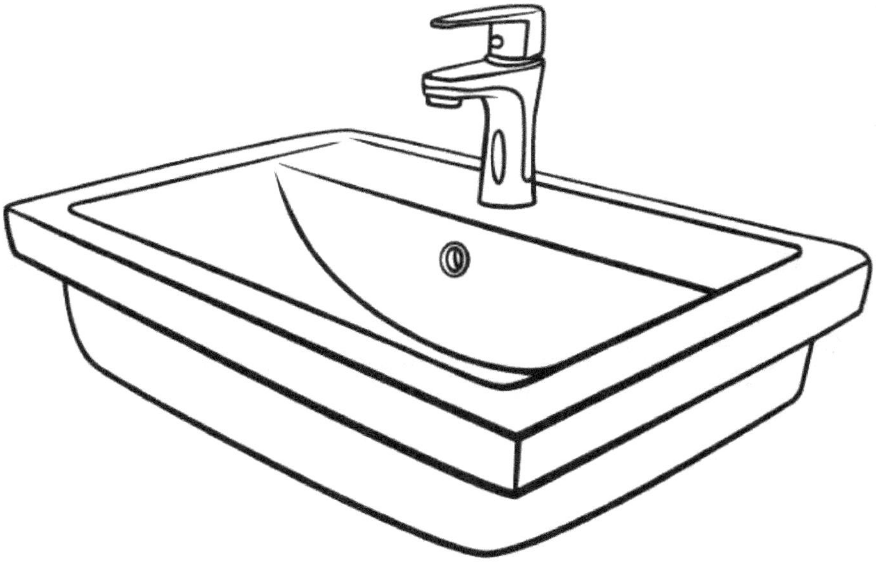

My name is

....

My name is

....

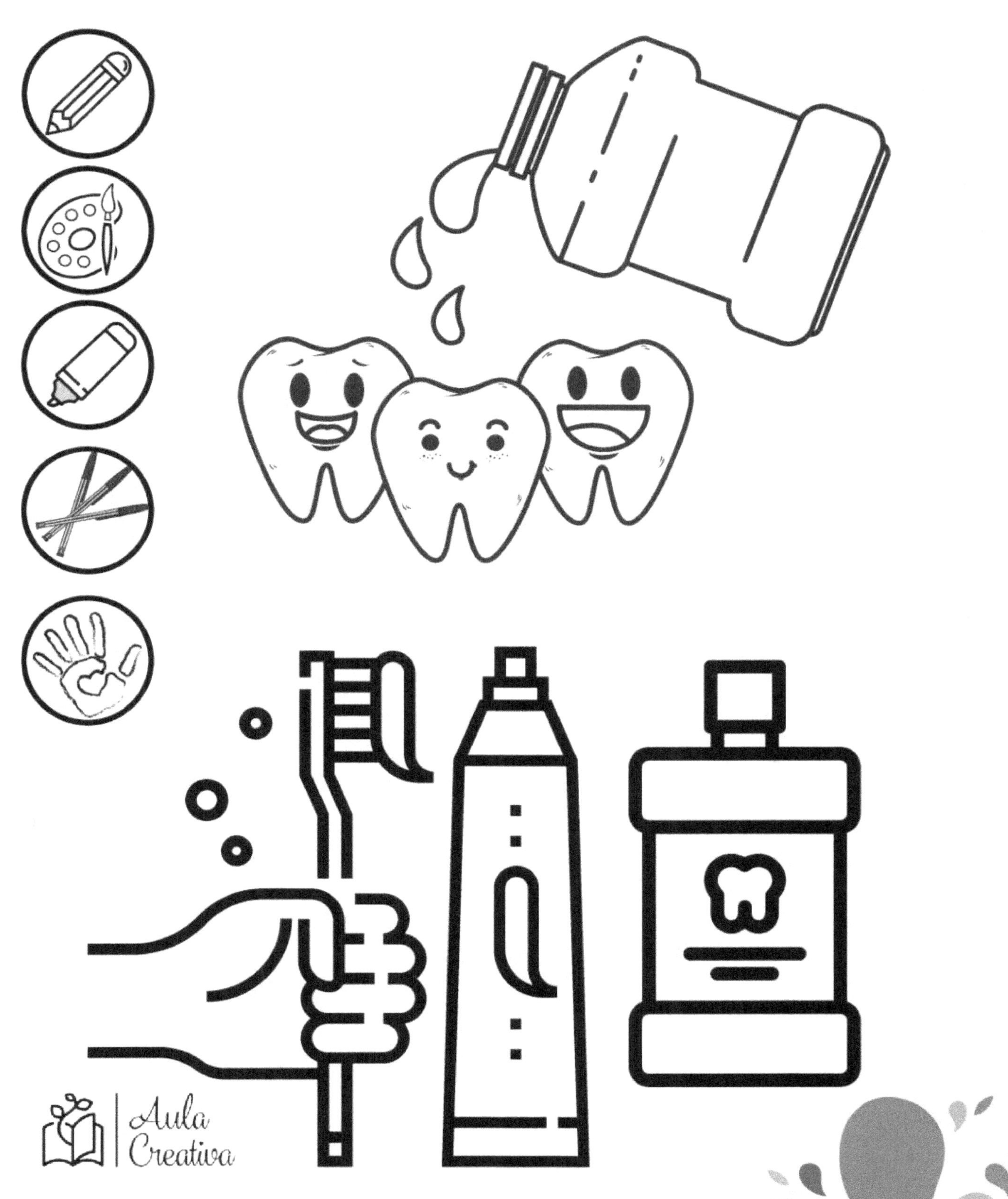

The Universe

....

Aula
Creativa

My name is
Earth
Aula Creativa

My name is

....

Aula Creativa

My name is

....

....

My name is

....

My name is

....

My name is

....

My name is

....

My name is

....

My name is

My name is

....

Mars

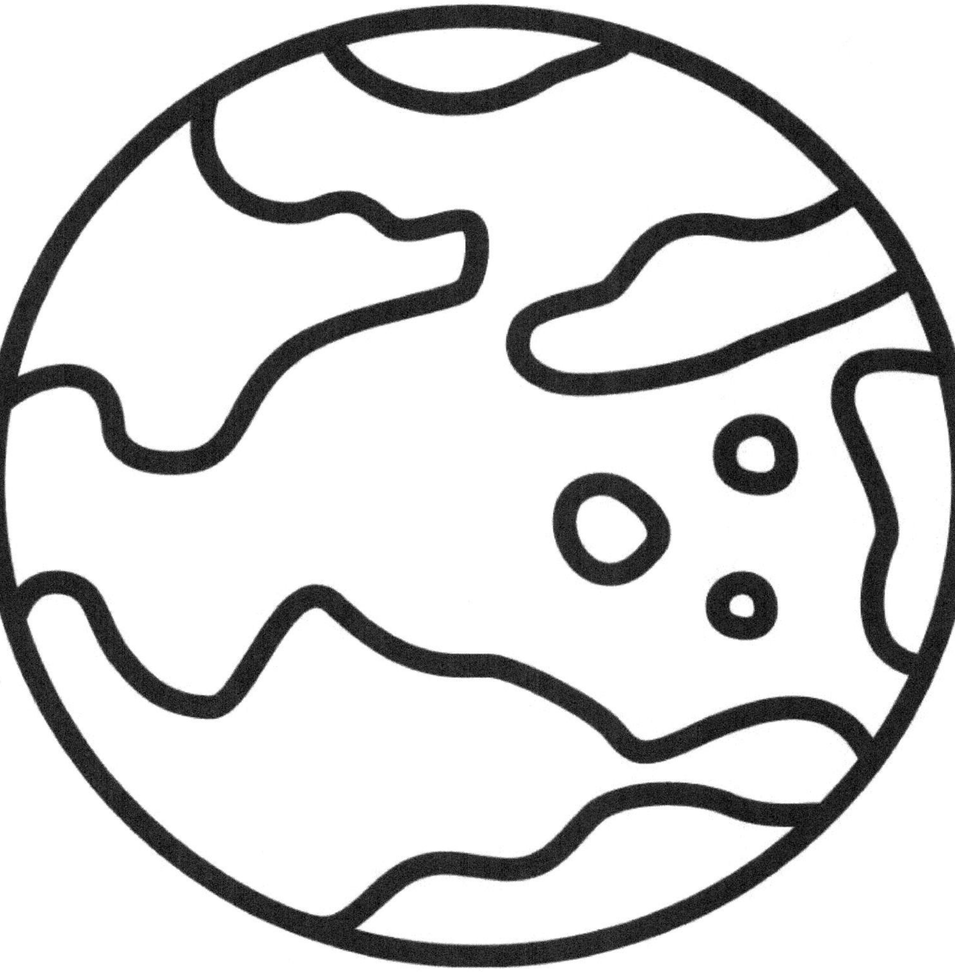

Venus

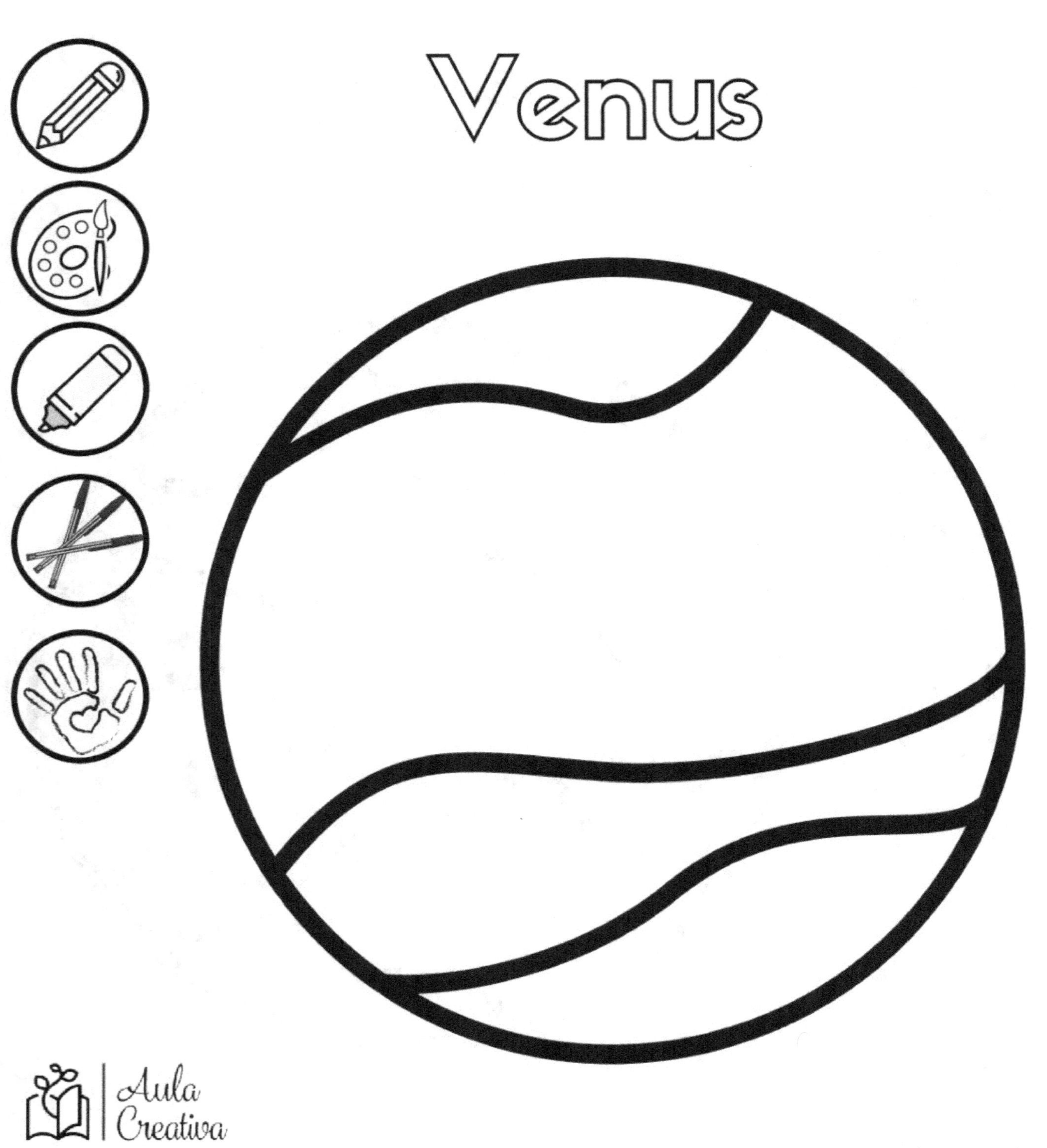

·····································

Saturn

My name is

....

Jupiter

Neptune
Aula
Creativa

Mercury

Pluto

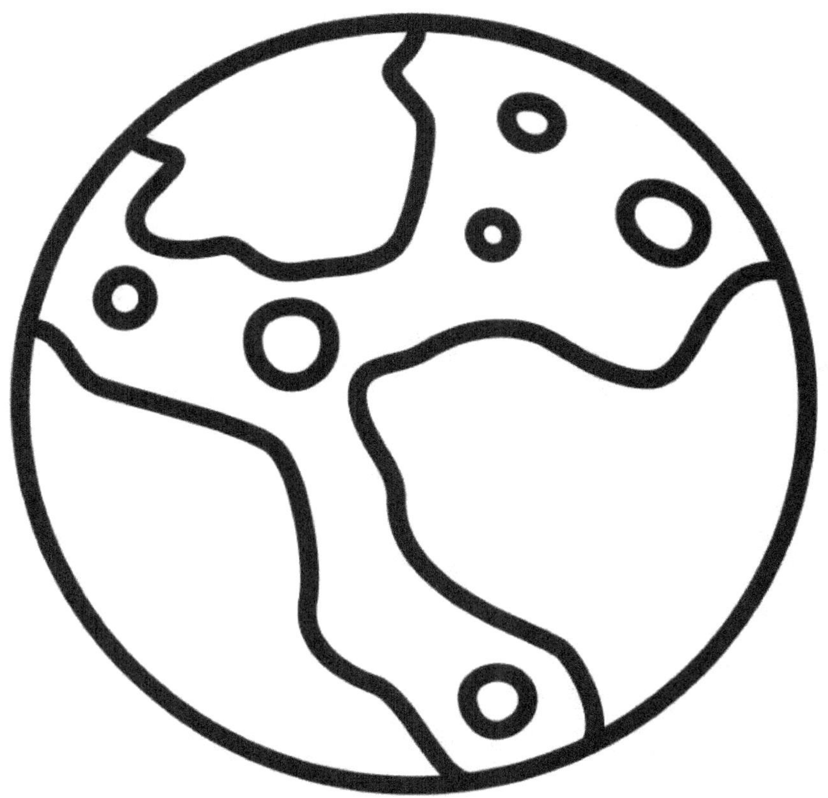

Aula
Creativa

My name is

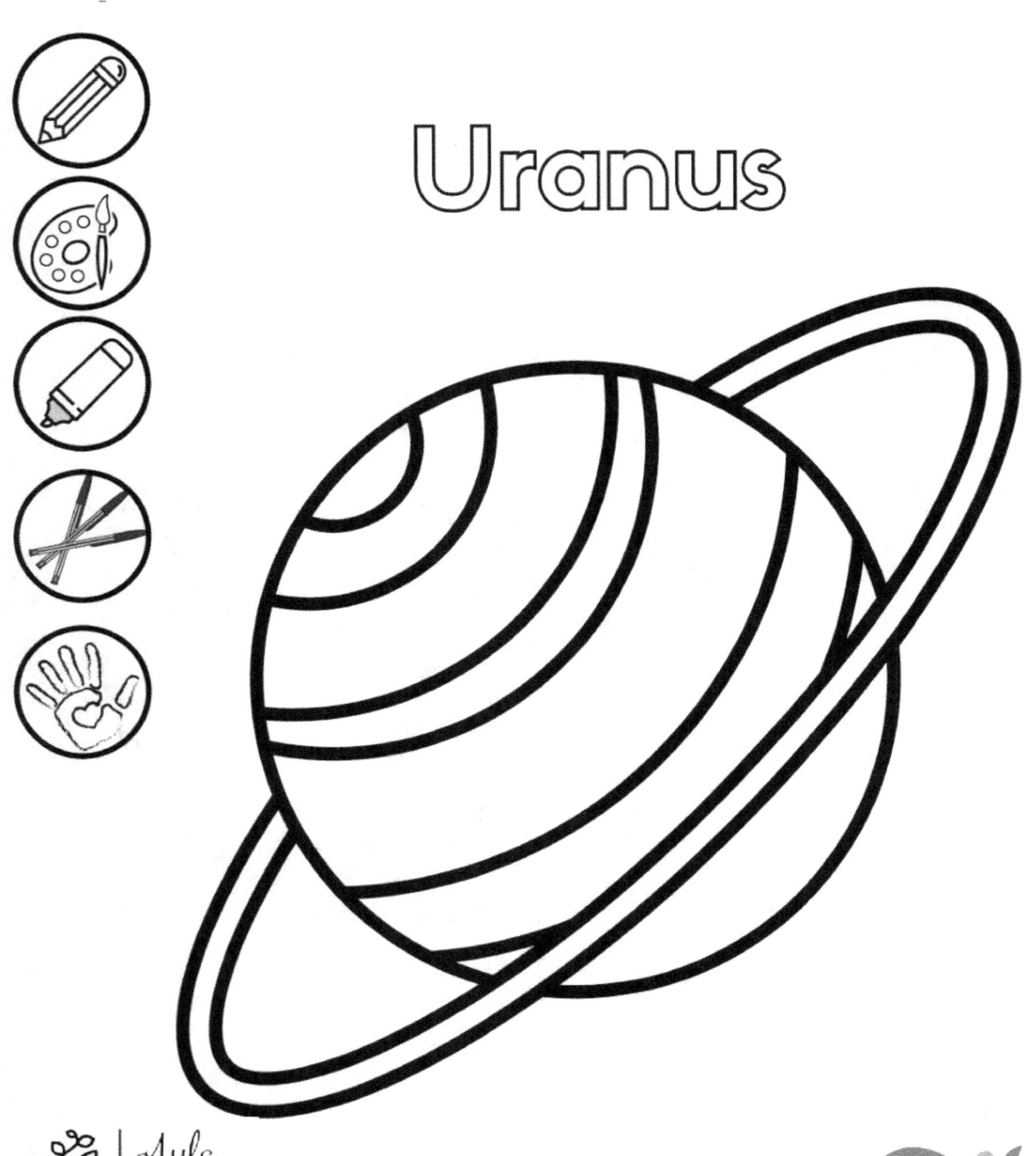

Uranus

My name is

My name is

....

My name is

My name is

Take care of the Earth

Aula Creativa

My name is

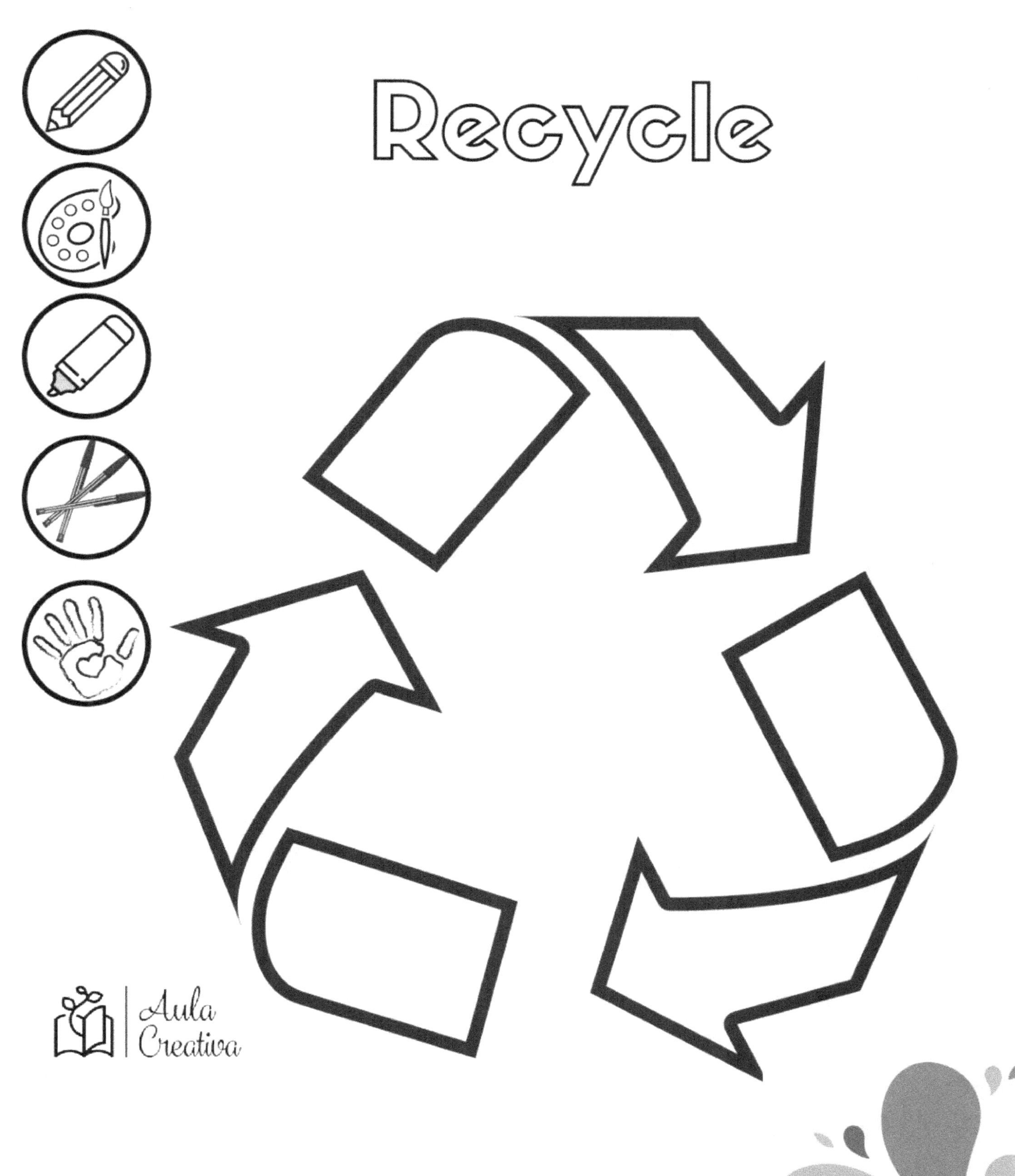
Recycle
Aula Creativa

My name is

Recycle

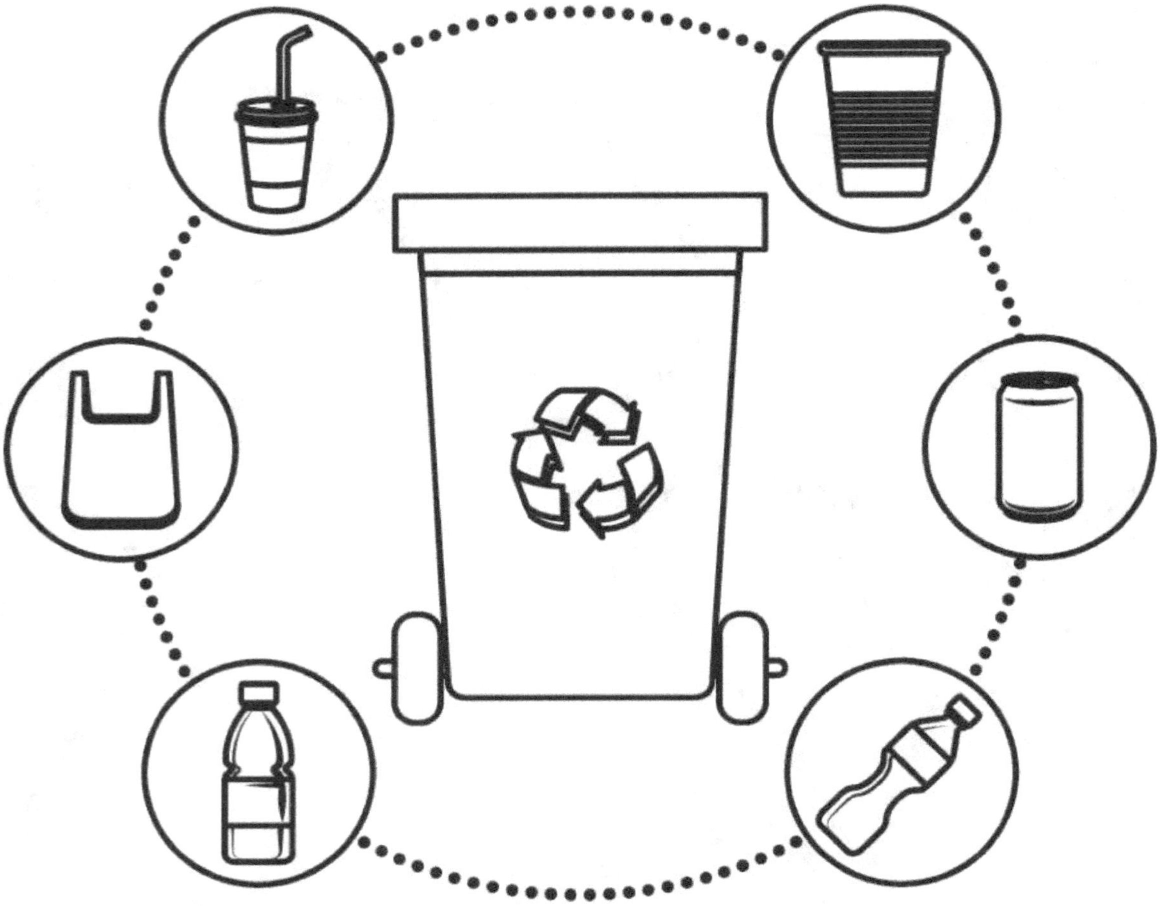

My name is

....

Recycle

Aula Creativa

My name is

....

My name is

....

My name is

....

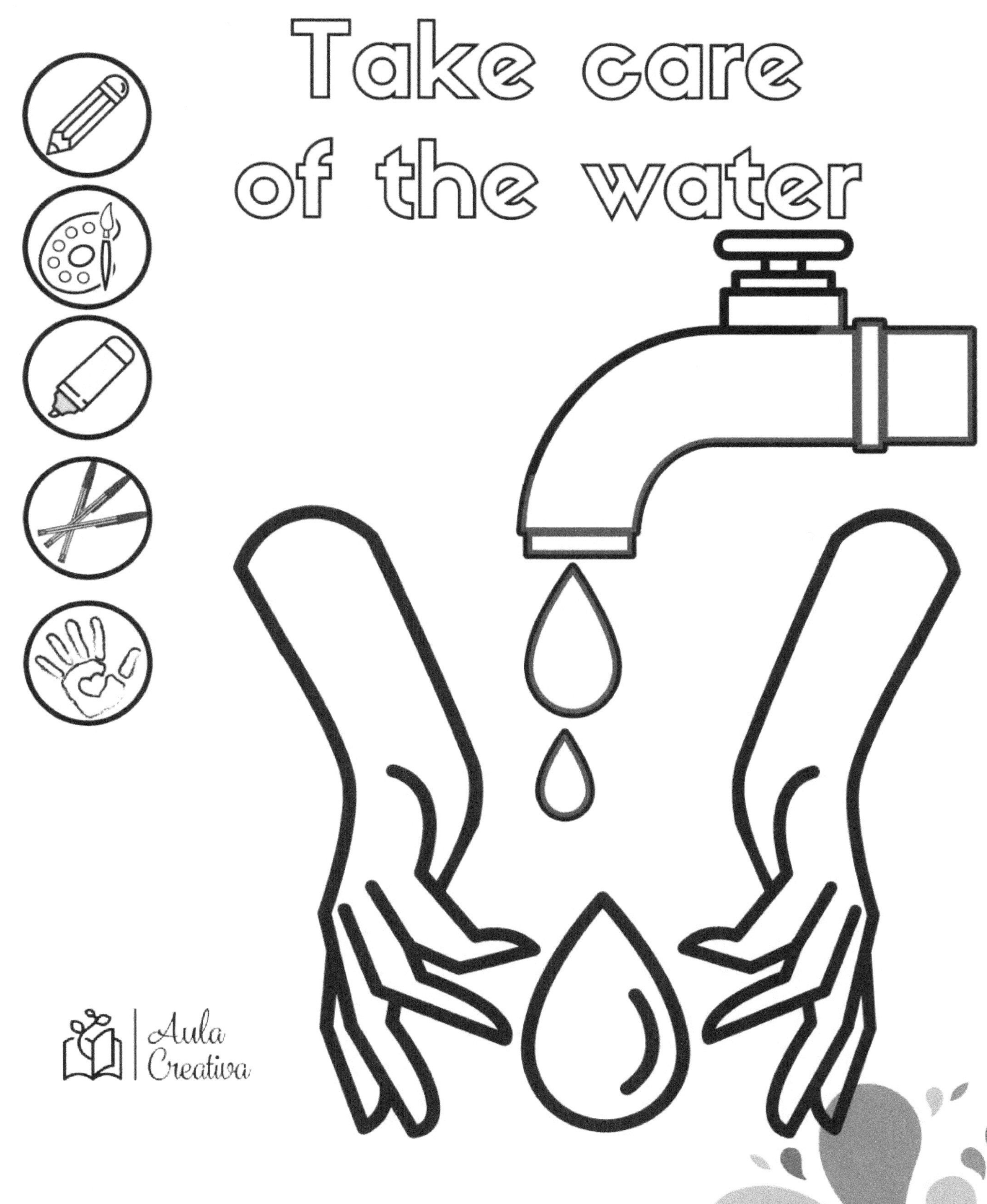

Take care
of the water
Aula
Creativa